CW01670448

4. HOTWELLS

Explore Bristol

ON FOOT

EXPLOREWALKS UK

Julia Killingback and Michael Pascoe

4. HOTWELLS

Explore **Bristol**

EXPLOREWALKS UK

Map © Julia Killingback 2014

At the half-way stage, the Junction Lock / Pump House ferry stop, you have several options:

1. Walking the circular route

This includes some steps, a section along open dockside and one steep climb up the Zig-Zag path. Those with buggies may need help in lifting on steps.

This section may not be suitable for young children.

2. Return by ferry and bus

Take the ferry from the Junction Lock / Pump House ferry stop to Bristol city centre. This is a request stop. Wave to the ferry operator – don't miss the boat! At the city centre catch a bus or taxi back up to Clifton. Ask for the Clifton Village bus stop where your walk began.

3. Return by bus

Look at the map. There are bus stops along Hotwell Road near the Junction Lock / Pump House ferry. You can catch a bus from here directly up to Clifton. Ask for the Clifton Village bus stop. Buses also go from here to the city centre where you can connect with other destinations.

Hotwells

Full Circular Walk

Total distance approx. 4¼ miles/6.8 kms

Average time needed – 2½ hours

Downhill Walk Only

Total distance approx. 2 miles/3.25 kms

Average time needed – 1½ hours

(Please allow time for ferry and bus connections.)
During the winter months ferry services are less frequent.
For details see Ferry Companies on page 43.

Our walk description begins at the Clifton Village Bus Stop

See the map pages 2 and 3.
This stop is close to the junction of Boyce's Avenue with Clifton Down Road, near the pedestrian crossing.
OS Explorer map 154,
Sat Nav: Postcode BS8 4AF

Get there

By bus – From Temple Meads Station
– From Bristol City Centre
– From Bristol Bus Station (a nearby stop)
Ask for the Clifton Village Bus Stop.

By Open Top Bus This makes a circular tour of Bristol (from February to December). It stops at the Clifton Village Stop.
Seasonal information: www.citysightseeingbristol.co.uk

By taxi – ask to be set down near the Clifton Village Bus Stop in Clifton Down Road.

Please note
This is a circular walk, so you may choose to begin at any point on our route knowing that you will return to the same spot eventually.

This walk includes two nearby children's playgrounds.

Mobility impaired We are sorry that we cannot recommend all of this circular route due to the hilly terrain.However an interesting section IS on the flat. (See the map pages 2 and 3). You might choose to park South of the Cumberland Basin or at the nearby at the Create Centre. From here make your way to Dowry Square ,via Merchants Road. Cross Hotwell Road using the controlled crossing.Turn left towards Dowry Square (description on page 20). Then follow the Hotwells route, which includes the quays. Once you reach the Nova Scotia -the car parks are nearby.

THE QUIZ When you see a numbered question in the text STOP! Look for the question at the bottom of the page. You should be able to discover the answer from this spot. When you think you know it, turn over– the numbered answers are shown at the bottom of the NEXT page. GOOD LUCK!

FUN FACTS. Look out for the smiley face telling you more as you go along.

Welcome to Hotwells

For many centuries most of the local population lived along the banks of the River Avon, below the hamlet of Clifton on the hill. The district of Hotwells owes its name to a natural spring which emerged from the muddy river banks at the foot of the Avon Gorge between high and low tides. The water, which was not especially hot, just 20°C(76°F), had long been drunk by sailors as a hoped-for cure for scurvy, a disease caused by the lack of fresh fruit and vegetables on long sea voyages.

When the Society of Merchant Venturers, the powerful guild of Bristol merchants, became lords of the manor of Clifton in 1685, they licensed two of their members to build Hotwell House beside the river. The milky water was pumped to the house and sold at a penny a glass. Following a visit by Catherine of Braganza, King Charles II's queen, a popular spa quickly developed. Lodging houses were built and let at 16 shillings (80p) a week. Servants were lodged at half price. The entire area flourished, resulting in a building boom of fine terraces, often overlooking private shared gardens. A theatre, pleasure gardens and two riverside assembly rooms were established. Bristol's Hotwell complemented Bath spa - Bath being a winter resort and Bristol a summer one.

There were other springs in the area, hence the plural Hotwells, but these were never developed to the same extent. The spa water was even exported overseas, which helped boost Bristol's flourishing glass-making industry. Bristol Blue glass is still made.

▲ **Hotwells, with a view of the Avon Gorge** c.1730 British School

The Hotwells also enticed healthy visitors and the resort attracted the eighteenth-century jet set. Throughout the century, many of the royalty, nobility and celebrities of the day came to the spa. They included the writers Daniel Defoe, Jonathan Swift and Alexander Pope. Two novels written at the time had the Hotwells as their background, Fanny Burney's Evelina and Tobias Smollett's Humphry Clinker. The poet Gray, playwright Sheridan and composer Haydn also came to take the waters.

Outdoor amusements were popular. Those who were healthy enough took carriages up to the hamlet of Clifton or to the open countryside of Clifton Downs. Here they could watch a game of cricket or bet on horse races. Wrestling and cock-fighting were especially popular with the gentlemen. Another pastime was to take a boat across the River Avon to enjoy strawberry teas in the beautiful Somerset countryside.

All that is now left of this glittering scene is a colonnade of former shops and lodgings. By the beginning of the nineteenth century the spa needed major improvements. A new Hotwells House was built by the Merchant Venturers in 1822 in the same spot. To recoup their investment, the price for drinking the water went up sharply. This drove away those attending just for pleasure and the spa became a last resort for invalids, giving Hotwells a sinister reputation. The Bristol- born poet Robert Southey describes the patients as *crawling out on to the tree-lined promenade as if to take their last gasp of sunshine.*

With sea bathing becoming popular at this time and new spas such as Cheltenham developing in the early nineteenth century, Hotwells declined further. The Pump Room was finally demolished in 1867 but the spring water was piped to a cavern at the foot of the cliff for local use. This outlet can still be seen near the Colonnade.

Contamination finally caused this source to be closed for good on health grounds in 1913.

▲ **Granby Hill, Clifton**
c.1822
Lt. Col. William Booth
(1748-1826)

As the Hotwells spa declined, the houses that had been built for visitors became tenements for poor people. By the beginning of the twentieth century there was massive overcrowding, often with five or more people to a room. Many of those who were able to find employment worked in the docks, in local factories, or as servants to the wealthy residents of newer Clifton up the hill.

Slum clearance began in the early twentieth century and enemy bombing during the Second World War (1939-1945) also took its toll of Hotwells. In the 1960s a large section of riverside Hotwells was demolished in order to build the Cumberland Basin road system. Despite this, during the 1950s and '60s, some far-sighted young families began buying the cheap, almost derelict, but fine Georgian houses, and brought them back to life. Bristol Docks were closed to commercial shipping in the 1970s. Recent years have seen the Hotwells area restored to life with much new development and it is now home to a vibrant community.

Facing the Clifton Village bus stop on Clifton Down Road, turn left and cross the entrance to Boyce's Avenue. Leaving the pedestrian crossing to your right, walk on down the left-hand pavement.

On your left you will see stately Boyces Buildings. In its pediment is the monogram of Thomas Boyce, a wigmaker, who had this built in 1763 as lodgings for visitors to the Hotwell spa.

➔ Cross the junction with Merchants Road and start to walk down Regent Street. After the corner office buildings, the first shop on your left has kept its original Victorian frontage. Stop here to see the curved sweep of the brick-built street, once famous for its 1870s Edwardian store, Cordeux.

➔ Now cross the road to Georgian Royal York Crescent. You can see over the door of the corner shop – 52 Royal York Crescent, painted in Victorian times. Just here the railings are supported by what was once an unusually small gas lamp, perhaps a very early experimental form.

Question 1 ***Look at the bottom of this page.***

OPTION

If you might have difficulty with a long flight of steps down at the far end of the level Crescent, you could choose to go to the end and back before following the Lower Route – Royal York Crescent. The lower route provides a different aspect of this massive terrace. For either of these choices you may wish to read the description of the Upper Route – Royal York Crescent on page 11 as far as Meeting Point.

Lower Route – Royal York Crescent (no steps). Continue along the lower right-hand pavement below the Crescent. When you reach the gardens, cross the road to the left-hand pavement. Go along by the original Georgian railings decorated with cast iron urns.

Question 1

Do you like going to the beach? Look at the lamp. What can you see that reminds you of it?

TURN OVER FOR ANSWERS

▲ **Royal York Crescent**
1791 - 1820
William Paty, Architect

As you proceed you can imagine the comings and goings at this level – cooks, maids, and footmen would have used these entrances. Notice how the roadway widens towards the centre of the Crescent to allow vehicles to turn more easily. Household goods and food would have been delivered by horse and cart or on a barrow. The trees in the private garden below you include a Mulberry and a Wellingtonia, just over thirty years-old and already tall.

When you approach the end of the lower route, cross the main road to the pavement close to the entrance to the Paragon, another curved terrace ahead.

Meeting Point – entrance to The Paragon.

Upper Route – Royal York Crescent (steps down at the far end).

➔ Walk along the start of the pavement at the beginning of the Crescent. Stop where it widens to take in the vista. Then walk on and enjoy looking at the individual houses. It is claimed to be Europe's longest crescent. Each house has four floors, a basement and a sub-basement. The balcony of Number 40 displays some intricate ironwork.

Number 25 was the home of Field Marshal Earl Roberts (*1832-1914*). He was Commander-in-Chief of the British Army during the Boer War in South Africa (*1899-1902*). Number 22 has a beautiful fanlight (fan-shaped window) over the door and a plaque giving a brief history of the Crescent.

Look up at the twisted barley-sugar design of the old drain pipe between Numbers 17 and 16. (There is an Italian pasta like this called fusilli). **Question 2**

Stop by the railings near the long flight of steps down at the far end of the Crescent to enjoy the splendid view over Bristol and beyond, and the fine gardens and terrace of the curved **Paragon** to your right.

Look at the grand Number 2, *Eugenie House*. The Empress Eugénie (*1825-1920*) future wife of Napoleon III (*1808-1873*) attended school here, apparently reluctantly, before moving to France. **Question 3**

Go down the steps to road level. Cross the road to the opposite pavement.

Meeting Point – entrance to the Paragon

Now you can look back up at the imposing Crescent topped off with the decorative urns of *Eugenie House*. Keeping to the right-hand pavement, walk downhill beside the curving wall of the garden. Pause when you reach the post box. To your right, the top of the wall beside the lane is made of unusual pointed bricks. Look down at the curious wedge-shaped house, a former shop, at the top of

Answer 1

A shell.

Question 2

What tasty fruits hang from the balcony?

Granby Hill. To your left you will see the sweeping curve of Cornwallis Crescent, begun in 1791 but not finished until about 1835. It was originally called the *Lower Crescent*. Beyond it you will see an old cast-iron sign saying To Windsor Terrace. Follow this direction along the right-hand pavement of **Windsor Place** and enjoy the view. **Question 4**

You will pass a south-facing garden to your right. Look up to an exotic-looking cliff-side garden and above that the magnificent Paragon, built between 1809 and 1814. The grandest residence contained a magnificent ballroom with panoramic views in both directions over the River Avon.

▲**The Paragon**, Built in five years by John Drew.

Question 3

Look up at Number 2. There are lots of grapes hanging from the balcony. Who can you spot nearby who might like to eat them?

Question 4

Look at the tops of the pillars outside Number 2 Windsor Place across the road. Why are they unusual?

Ahead of you is **Windsor Terrace**. Walk between its elegant cast-iron gateposts. The terrace was begun in 1793 by William Watts, a Bristol plumber. He had an idea that was supposed to have come to him in a dream. It involved dropping molten lead through a screen from a 27 metre (90 foot) tower into a tank of water at its base. This rendered the drops into perfect spheres – lead shot, which is still in use for shot gun cartridges to this day. He made a fortune which he invested in constructing this terrace, but the scheme bankrupted him. The houses were completed later to a much less ambitious design than originally planned. Walk along the terrace and continue to the far end for an exciting view.

Wild flowers have seeded themselves towards the edge of the terrace. They include the Mexican daisy, ox-eye daisy, wallflower, spreading bellflower and Icelandic poppy.

A former resident at Number 4 was Hannah More (*1745-1833*) author, feminist, playwright and friend of Dr Johnson (*1709-1784*). The old hand-cut cobbles were so well matched that they could be laid without cement. You will see square coal holes set into the roadway. The coal cellars for these houses are under the road. Beneath them are even more layers of cellars.

At Number 1 a plaque commemorates Edward St John Daniel who was born here and won the Victoria Cross in the Crimean War aged 17. He was later ordered to forfeit the medal after being drunk, absent without leave and finally deserting – the only VC having to give up his medal.

→ Cross to the terrace edge. Look over the side. You will appreciate how massive the supporting wall is, built without the benefit of modern machinery. Constructing the huge foundations 21 metres (70 feet) right out into the gorge was an incredibly daring project for its time.

Looking out, you can see Bristol Docks entrance. Across the river is wooded Rownham Hill, and beyond it, Ashton Court Estate, now a beautiful and extensive park open to the public.

Answer 2

Grapes.

Answer 3

Six greedy cast-iron birds are waiting to eat them.

Look up at the skyline beyond Bristol. The church tower that you see is that of Dundry.

▲ **Windsor Terrace**
1793-1816
John Eveleigh of Bath
Architect (attributed)

➔ Make your way back to the fine gates.

Before you leave the terrace look up at the wall of Number 10. Someone is sticking their tongue out at you. How rude!

➔ Take the road downhill. Only 50 years separate the building style of the Paragon towering above you from **Victoria Terrace** on your left. You will reach **Granby Hill**. Pause on this pavement by the road sign slightly up hill to your left. Look across at the corner house on Hope Chapel Hill. This is *Rutland House*, dating from about 1760.

How strange. You can't go in through this front door.

Option *For those unable to manage steps, cross the road and continue a little way down Hope Chapel Hill.*

Meeting Point – entrance to **Hope Square.**

Answer 4

The house address is neatly carved to show that the stonework belongs here.

Continuing the route. Cross Granby Hill to walk uphilll a short way only, on the right-hand side. Look up towards Number 52, the house with protruding steps and a Georgian lamp bracket. Eugénie, the future Empress of France, lived in this house while at school on Royal York Crescent above. Imagine climbing that hill every day.
Now look out for Number 48. **Question 5**

➔ Descend the steps. This is an unusual short cut leading to Hope Square.

Look at the Georgian brick houses on your left. The mortar between the bricks is very thin, measured by masons with the thickness of an oyster shell. This square was in a ruinous state in the 1950s and '60s. Most of the right-hand side had been bombed during the Second World War (1939-1945) and was replaced by modern flats. Fortunately, the upper terrace survived.

At Number 11 there is a plaque to scientist Dr Beddoes (*1760-1808*). He had a laboratory in this house before he moved further down the hill. You will read more about him later. There is a sundial on Number 14. Standing here you can appreciate the great skill of the Georgian carpenters who made the finest of glazing bars for windows. Leaving the modern flats to your right, walk down to the entrance of the Square.

Meeting Point – entrance to **Hope Square**.

➔ Turn left down **Hope Chapel Hill**. Across the road is the nineteenth-century brick-built *Hotwells Primary School* with its striking polychromatic decoration in stone and brick. The 1960s fashion designs of Mary Quant (born 1934) had a similar look!

➔ Cross Hope Chapel Hill to the left-hand pavement of Georgian **Albemarle Row**. Pause here. The houses opposite have unusually large keystones over the windows and extra-ordinarily decorative doorways.

Question 5

There is a secret by Number 48. What is it?

▲ Granby Hill

Just look at the size of the front door of Number 1. It's huge. Strangely enough a giant did once live near here. 200 years ago a very tall man – 2m 46cm (8ft 1ins) lived in Hotwells. He was so tall that he could light his pipe from the gas flame at the top of a lamp post in his street.

➔ Walk on to the central house of this terrace. It has a pediment with the monogram of its owner, *John Webb*, and the date of the terrace, 1763.

➔ Retrace your steps. Pause at the corner. Look across the road to *Hope Chapel*. This was the joint project of friends Lady Glenorchy (*1741-1786*) and Lady Hope (*1750-1786*). Sadly neither lived to see the chapel's completion in 1788. It has been used in recent years as the Hotwells Community Centre, and has now reverted almost entirely to church use. Visitors are welcome.

➔ Take small **Polygon Lane** past the bollards, alongside Hope Chapel. Walk along the footpath to **The Polygon**. Stop at the top of the steps which go down to it and read on.

A God-fearing Place

Hope Chapel for the Congregationalists, Grenville Chapel for the Methodists, Buckingham Chapel for the Baptists, Cumberland Hall for the Brethren, Trinity Church and Dowry Chapel for the Anglicans plus seven mission halls run by a variety of denominations. Local women depended on church for their social life.

This is one of Hotwells' most hidden and enchanting terraces. Unlike the convex Cornwallis Crescent above it, this terrace is concave. It was built around about 1830. Apart from the pretty individual front gardens, the residents share the large communal garden above it. Look up towards the top right-hand corner of the garden where you will see an unusual tulip tree. In winter, above you between the trees, you can see the back of Cornwallis Crescent with its remarkable shared broad terraced walk.

➔ Continue along the path close to the Polygon houses.

Option. *If you cannot manage nearby steps down, take the upper path above the communal garden. You will have a beautiful view of The Polygon below, framed by the trees of the garden. Continue to the junction and turn right down the sloping lane to the far end of The Polygon.*

Meeting Point – far end of The Polygon.

➔ Go down **Polygon Lane South**, past the old bollards. As you go into **North Green Street**, pause to look up at the backs of The Polygon. Before mains water was available, people depended on earth closets for toilets. These were emptied by *night-soil men* with buckets who made a living selling excrement as manure. Today the sewage works at Avonmouth sells treated sewage sludge for the same purpose. Once mains water was laid on in the 1850s, a variety of bathroom and kitchen extensions were added piecemeal to the backs of the houses. You may have noticed Georgian architects avoided ugly drain pipes at the front.

Look at the unusual curved corner building with its pretty Gothic-style windows, probably a former gatehouse.

There is a tiny window in a door at street level. It looks like a miniature coach house.

You pass the ironically named *Albert Hall* (two houses) on your left. *The Adam and Eve* pub, at the corner with Granby Hill, dates from about 1775. Turn left downhill.

Answer 5

Surprise, surprise – it's a secret passageway!

▲ **The Adam and Eve**
Built c.1775

At the bottom of the hill cross right. Look up at the house on the corner – Number 262 – built in the 1720s. It has pretty chequer-board brickwork and one of Bristol's earliest fanlights above the door. ● **Question 6**

Look across at Dowry Parade with its fine row of Plane trees. In 1762 the Society of Merchant Venturers granted leases to build these as lodging houses. Individual rooms or floors were let, probably to lodgers visiting the Hotwells Spa. The ownership reverted to the Society when the leases expired.

Now cross the bottom of Hope Chapel Hill again. Pause at the corner. The black coping stones supporting the railings around the gardens, the main road end of **Dowry Square**, were made from compressed slag, a by-product of copper, manufactured in the 1700s near Bristol. Look out for more of this feature on your walks.

● **Question 6**

What can you see above the windows? How many are there? How old do you think they are?

Around Dowry Square

Walk along the left-hand side of the square. Building began in the 1720s but was not completed until the 1750s. Each house was constructed as an individual project rather than as part of an overall scheme. These were the earliest lodgings to be built for visitors to the nearby Hotwell spa. At that time this whole area would have been bustling with people.

Question 7

Dr Thomas Beddoes used the unusual L-shaped corner house, Number 6, as his laboratory and established a Pneumatic Institution. You can read the plaque.

Can you imagine a cow being driven up the steps into one of these fine houses? This is what is supposed to have happened 200 years ago. A local doctor thought that if cows breathed on them it would make his sick patients better.

Dr Beddoes was looking for a cure for tuberculosis, then called consumption, rife at that time. The cow experiment seemed extreme and landladies were naturally not amused. Beddoes was not mad. He had noticed that slaughterhouse workers and butchers seemed less susceptible to tuberculosis than others, and perhaps working closely with animals might be the reason.

Beddoes hired 19-year-old Humphry Davy (*1778-1829*) as his apprentice and it was while working here that Davy discovered nitrous oxide (laughing gas) which later formed the basis of modern anaesthetics. Davy's friends included the poets Samuel Taylor Coleridge (*1772-1834*) and Robert Southey (*1774-1843*) who both tried out the gas. Southey said: *Davy has invented a pleasure for which the language has no name. He described the sensation as laughing in every toe and fingertip!* Number 6 also bears a plaque to Sir Humphry Davy who also invented the miner's safety lamp.

Question 8

Answer 6

Masks. There are 14. They are nearly 300 years old and some are still smiling.

Beddoes

Davy

Coleridge

Southey

▲ **Dowry Square**
c.1721-1746 George Tully, Carpenter

Other noteable early nineteenth-century residents of Dowry Square were Peter Mark Roget (*1779-1869*), another local doctor, who created Roget's Thesaurus, and Jacob Schweppe (*1740-1821*) a Swiss who came to Bristol to manufacture Hotwell water impregnated with air – using carbon dioxide to produce a fizzy drink. His name is now familiar worldwide. Number 7 has a broken pediment over the door and Number 8 has an intricate Queen Anne style shell hood porch. Look at Number 10. ● **Question 9**

The door knocker shows a hand-held scroll. A fine old Wisteria grows here. Number 12 has an iron bracket, from which a sign once hung. Pause. Look up at Number 13. *Clifton Dispensary* is carved in the stonework. Established in 1823, this building has an air of importance with its double flight of steps and additional side windows which give more light inside the building. Here, the dispensary doctors did their best to care for the wealthy but often ailing visitors to the Hotwell. The fees paid by these patients allowed some of the more public-spirited amongst them to provide free medical care for the local sick and poor – a kind of early National Health Service.

● Question 7

Look at Number 2. Who once worked here?

● Question 8

Look at the door knocker of Number 6. What can you see?

● Question 9

Read the words on the marble plate to the left of the door. What do they say?

Dowry Square and Hotwell Road

Numbers 14 and 15 have delicate fanlights.

There are some unusual trees in Dowry Square gardens – a Bull Bay tree (which is an evergreen Magnolia) from South Carolina and an Arizona Cypress which is uncommon.

In winter look out for an Azara, a small tree brought to England from South America. Over there it flowers in their hot summertime but because our seasons are the opposite of South America's, here the little Azara still bravely flowers even though it's our chilly winter.

Nearing Hotwell Road, you will pass bow-fronted *York House*, once a hotel. Look for the old iron edging to the pavement here. This is common in Bristol. The edge prevented the iron-bound carriage wheels from damaging the stone kerb. Pause at the corner. Look across the road at the blank side of the last house of Dowry Parade. **Question 10**

Before modern central heating the only way to keep warm was to light coal fires in every room. Imagine how tired the poor servants must have been, shovelling coal stored in the cellars, then carrying the heavy buckets up all those stairs, perhaps several times a day!

➔ Leaving Dowry Square, turn left along the pavement of **Hotwell Road**. Continue along. On your left you will pass the brick-built *Hillsborough Flats*, a large council development of 1935, a type that is quite rare in Bristol.

In the heyday of the Bristol docks this road was lined with busy shops. There were at least 35 pubs and other premises to please the homecoming sailors. Unsurprisingly, it was then called Love Street. Look across the road to see the original bay and bow windows of the shops at Numbers 267 and 265. You can also see the Georgian Bear pub with its carriage yard entrance. Behind this would have been stables. Cross the bottom of steep Clifton Vale. Pause in front of the church.

Answer 7

Mr Robert Young, a surgeon who performed operations 200 years ago

Answer 8

A swan.

▲ **Holy Trinity Church**
c.1830 Charles Cockerell Architect

This was designed in 1830 by Charles Cockerell (*1788-1863*) well-known as the architect of Britain's first public museum, the Ashmolean in Oxford. It was the last church in the classical style to be built in Bristol. The carved dove represents the Holy Spirit. In Victorian times the church was much needed by the then fast-growing population of Hotwells. In those days Sundays were days set aside for worship and for rest. During the Second World War the building suffered severe bomb damage and the interior had to be completely rebuilt. Visitors are welcome to Sunday worship.

➔ Cross the road here at the light-controlled pedestrian crossing to the central reservation. Turn sharp right and cross again. You will reach a small fountain in the corner between two buildings. This commemorates Simon Short (*1848- 1901*). An inscription on the plaque gives details of his work as a preacher to seamen. He also founded an anti-alcohol movement, which encouraged people to forsake pubs and to drink in cocoa and coffee taverns instead. ● **Question 11**

Answer 9

This was the bell to ring if you got back very late from a jolly evening out at the Hotwells spa. On the right the bell marked **House** was for daytime use.

● **Question 10**

Look up! How many chimney pots are there?

● **Question 11**

Look for cocoa beans on the fountain. Find Simon Short! Describe two things about him.

For nearby playground see the map.

➔ Now return to the central reservation. Turn right (away from the church). Pause here to look right at the 1839 Merchants Arms pub. It was named after the Society of Merchant Venturers, Bristol's guild of merchants, influential in Bristol commercial success for several centuries. Cross the main road at the light-controlled crossing, turn left and immediately right into quieter **Rownham Mead**, completed in 1973. Make your way, keeping left, towards the older stone building ahead of you. This is a nineteenth-century dockside warehouse. Reaching the far side of it, you can see its hoist still in place.

➔ Turn right, towards the arched road entrance of Poole's Wharf Court, a 1990s development. Go through the pedestrian entrance and walk straight on. You will reach an alleyway which brings you out on to the dockside. Please be aware of safety notices in this area. **Stop here by the water to read the next section**.

Thomas L. S. Rowbottom 1823-1875

Since earliest times Bristol's wealth was founded on the success of its inland and overseas trade which brought great riches to the city. Bristol was Britain's second largest port after London for much of the eighteenth century. Originally, the River Avon was tidal right up into the centre of the city which is to your left. This caused huge problems. When the tide ebbed, sailing ships became stranded on the mud which often damaged their timbers. It was not until 1809 that William Jessop (*1745-1815*) constructed a huge lock which effectively closed off the river. This meant an extensive dock, with a controllable water level, known as the *Floating Harbour* could be built and ships could at last be loaded and unloaded around the clock. However, with the advent of larger ships, new more accessible docks, were constructed at Avonmouth, Portishead and later Portbury.

Sadly, these once busy city docks were finally closed to commercial shipping in the 1970s. They are now used in a

Answer 10

There are 25. In Georgian times central heating had not yet been invented. To keep warm a coal fire was lit in every room.

Answer 11

Well done if you found it and saw that he wore glasses and had a beard.

more leisurely way. Many events take place here throughout the year including a Harbour Festival, Dragon Boat races and University rowing regattas. You might see a fisherman landing a roach, dace or even a carp.

▲ Poole's Wharf

Look across the harbour. The land you see is called *Spike Island* and is part of Hotwells. Its 1990s development is built on the former *Baltic Wharf* where timber was once landed.

Question 12

In summer, you might spot house martins darting around *Poole's Wharf*. They nest under the eaves of the houses. Grey wagtails, with grey backs, yellow breasts and long tails flit around the quays here too.

Baltic Wharf 1938

Now walk right, along the dockside towards the pedestrian bridge. This particular area was once the landing wharf for sand dredged out in the Bristol Channel and shipped here to be processed for the building trade. Stop on the footbridge. At the far end of this inlet, called *Poole's Wharf Marina*, you can see the warehouse we passed earlier. Look up and enjoy the splendid view of Royal York Crescent along the skyline.

Question 12

Can you see what decorates the weather vanes on the roofs?

Shipshape and Bristol fashion

A well-known phrase probably linked to Bristol's once tidal harbour. Ships built here then were extra strong to withstand the pull of the outgoing tide which left them stranded high and dry on the mud.

Leaving the bridge you can see historic *Underfall Yard* across the water. Still housed in these buildings is a system designed by Isambard Kingdom Brunel (*1806-1859*) to pump the accumulating river silt out of the floating harbour. The yard is now an Industrial Heritage Site. Beyond it are some huge red-brick warehouses which will be described later. Continue along the dockside. Note the pretty gardens. Plants bloom here by the water much earlier than those at the top of the hill in Clifton. You will reach an inlet and the Pump House ferry stop.

○ **Pump House ferry/bus Option** You might choose to end your walk here – see the map pages 2 and 3.

Continuing the circular walk
The home stretch includes working locks, the site of the Hotwell spa, dramatic views of the Avon Gorge, Brunel's *Suspension Bridge* and the aptly-named *Zig-Zag* path that makes its way through woodland up the side of the gorge. There is much of historic interest. This section of the walk includes an invigorating climb and we should remember that walking is good for our hearts!

The walk continues on along the dockside. You will pass the brick walls indicating the former dock railway, then the first lock with its footbridge. On your right is the nineteenth century *Pump House* building, now a pub. Originally it housed a steam engine which provided the hydraulic pressure system to control the swinging bridges and the final massive lock gates to Bristol harbour which you will see shortly.

➔ Leaving the *Pump House* to your right, walk up the slope to **Merchants Road**. You are at Point Ⓐ on the map. Pause here. Close by you is the *1925 Junction Lock Swing Bridge*. Ahead is the huge holding area called *The Cumberland Basin* where ships wait to enter or leave the main harbour. Beyond that is the 1965 elevated *Plimsoll Swing Bridge*.

Answer 12
Sailing boats.

● **Question 13**
Look at the end wall of these buildings. When were the Docks Cottages built?

Having two bridges means that traffic can cross the harbour at all times even though ships are constantly navigating in and out of the dock area.

▲ **Dock Cottages** and the original dock into the harbour

As pedestrians, we have to accept that occasionally (but usually not for long) certain pedestrian crossing points may be closed to allow ships to pass or for safety reasons. If so, and you would prefer to keep walking, please see the map. Make your way from Point Ⓐ to Point Ⓑ. Our described route offers the best views.

→ Turn left to cross *Junction Lock bridge*. You will pass a plaque with details.At the far end of the bridge, you are on *Spike Island*. To your left, overlooking an outlet from the Underfall Yard, there is a terrace of old Dock Cottages built originally for retired employees of the Bristol Dock Company.

● **Question 13**

Ahead is the 1811 *Nova Scotia Hotel* with its original stable entrance. It was a popular hostelry for seafarers, dock workers and for the men herding beef cattle newly arrived from Ireland onto the nearby quays and destined for the Sunday lunch tables of Bristol.

Spoilt for Choice

In the mid-nineteenth century there were 32 pubs within one mile. Of these The Bear, the Plume of Feathers and the Adam and Eve date from the eighteenth century, whilst The Mardyke, The Spring Gardens, The Rose of Denmark, the Nova Scotia and the Merchant's Arms survive from the nineteenth century.

Now cross Merchants Road, taking the path down to the car park. Continue along the quayside. Look out for one of the four enormous anchors placed at each corner of this holding dock. **Question 14**

You will pass several mooring posts, their inscriptions reflect Bristol's past ironwork industry.

See if you can spot Royal York Crescent from here.

You are close to one of the massive tobacco bond buildings, built in the early 1900s. They were constructed as warehouses to store newly-imported tobacco from America until customs duty was paid. Tobacco was one of Bristol's major industries until the 1960s. The bricks hide an early example of a building using reinforced concrete. Today, Bristol City's archives are kept safely here and there is a thriving *Create Centre*. Look up! If you are lucky you might see kestrels flying – they nest on the lofty roofs and swoop around over the harbour. Continue safely towards another anchor and the road bridge beyond. Now look for a spiral staircase leading on to the road bridge. **Don't climb it. Pass under the bridge. Take the second spiral staircase on the far side and pause at the top.**
This bridge is named after Samuel Plimsoll (*1824-1898*) who invented the *Plimsoll Line*, an ingenious marking system painted on ships' hulls to prevent unscrupulous owners from overloading their vessels. You will see an amazing view over the harbour Entrance Lock and the tidal *River Avon*, also Windsor Terrace and the Paragon on the cliff side, and Isambard Kingdom Brunel's (*1806-1859*) famous *Suspension Bridge* straddling the Gorge 75 metres/245 feet above the river. Now walk along the *Plimsoll Bridge* towards this view. You will overlook Brunel's lesser known bridge beneath you – more details soon. Look out for Bristol's coat of arms attached to the railings. **Question 15**

➔ Take the next spiral staircase down to the *North Entrance Lock*. Please look out for the safety notices.

Answer 13
1831.

You have reached Point Ⓑ on the map. Pause here. Look across the lock. Now you are close to the 1849 hand-powered *Swivel Bridge*. The bridge is a wrought-iron, tubular design, which Brunel later used in his Chepstow and Saltash bridges. Originally it crossed the nearby *Southern Lock* which he also designed. The original roadways leading to it are still intact, as are the road gates. The massive new lock gates close to you are designed to hold the water in the harbour at a constant level. The gates can be opened only when the incoming tides rise bringing the river up to the same level as that of the water trapped within the harbour i.e. twice in every 24 hours.

▲ **North Entrance Lock** previously Howard's Lock *1873* and named after its engineer

▼ **Brunel's 1849 Swivel Bridge**

You now have two options

1. If the lock crossings are open to the opposite quay, and you are aware of the advice given, you might like to explore it, or 2. You may wish to continue your Hotwells walk straight away. Whatever your choice, you will see the same features.

Question 14

Look at the huge anchor. How much do you think it weighs?

Question 15

What creatures hold the shield?

Isambard Kingdom Brunel 1806-1859 by John Calcott Horsley 1817-1903

Continuing the circular walk. You are at **Point** Ⓑ on the map.
➔ Go up the few steps to **Cumberland Basin Road**.
Turn left in the direction of the pedestrian footbridge.
Look out for a capstan on the dockside opposite.
● **Question 16** and ● **Question 17**

You will see the Dock Master's *Watch House* – the larger building. (Two Dock Masters share work around the clock to ensure the efficient running of the harbour.) The smaller building beyond it, unsurprisingly called the *Leaning Tower*, contained the mechanisms to control the level of water within the dock. The water levels in feet are carved into the stone walls beside the final lock gates between the harbour and the *River Avon*.

Paddle Steamer Waverley

Climb the footbridge. Stop when you reach the first corner at the top of the steps to enjoy the view.

During the summer season, the steamship Balmoral ties up here to unload and load her cheerful passengers. The boats offer a pleasant cruise through the *Avon Gorge* and on downriver to the Bristol Channel, South Wales, north Somerset and Devon coasts. In past times ships departing from the docks under sail had to navigate the entire length (9 km/6 miles) of the gorge. The twists of the Avon, the tricky winds and changing tides all presented an unusual and challenging passage.

If you are lucky you may spot a heron on the muddy riverbanks – a tall grey bird with very large wings. Looking beyond the river, especially in the evenings, you may hear rooks and jackdaws and see them circling over the trees. Spiralling overhead you may see herring gulls, with their grey backs, also lesser black-backed gulls. Both have brown young. In winter, black-headed gulls (small, with bright red beaks and legs) can be seen here too. To your right at road level the L-shaped house close by once belonged to a sea captain. Cross the bridge. At the far end as you walk down, on your left is an interesting old shop front.

Answer 14

192 cwt (hundredweight) = 9.7 tonnes – about the same weight as a grown elephant! Thomas Bewick Woodcut *c* 1790

Answer 15

Two unicorns – not real beasts but magical ones.

Following the steps climb up **Granby Hill** a short way and turn left into **Freeland Place**. The 1820s colourful stepped houses have pretty iron balconies. **Question 18**

Samuel Jackson (*1794-1869*) one of the early nineteenth-century Bristol School of Artists, lived at Number 3.

▲ Freeland Place
Built *c.*1822

Look at the garden of Number 3. There is a topiary bird – you won't find him in a bird book.

Number 4 has a stylish Regency porch and fanlight. Number 7 has a Georgian lamp over the front door. Samuel Jackson later moved down the road to Number 8. Look at the swirling Art Nouveau tops of the gate supports at Number 22 to your left. Number 18 has an original bow window.

At the bottom of Freeland Place turn right. This is noisy **Hotwell Road**. It leads to the Portway, linking Bristol and the port at Avonmouth. It took seven years to build and provided work for the unemployed after the First World War (*1914-1918*). When it opened in 1926 it was the most expensive road ever to be built in Britain, costing £800,000.

Question 16

What are capstans used for?

Question 17

What kind of guns are on the quay either side of the lock?

Question 18

Who reigns over the entrance of Number 2?

Passing Hinton Lane look up at the towering cliff above you and the vast bulk of Windsor Terrace, from which you looked down earlier. Look towards the river and the derelict quays. These were busy with day-trippers in the 1920s and 30s catching paddle steamers to Clevedon, Cardiff or Ilfracombe. The cliffs are even more impressive from river level.

You come to *St Vincent's Parade*. Walk along. This Georgian terrace begun in 1789, was then approached by a pretty tree-lined walk. The painter Rolinda Sharples (*1793-1838*) lived at Number 372. (See her painting on page 34.) The last house, Number 388A, is a replica. Note the Victorian post box.

➔ Continue past the Edwardian houses. Number 412, *Rock House,* of about 1740, predates the Georgian Colonnade ahead. It has double doors, an attractive fanlight and two storeys of balconies reminiscent of those in New Orleans.

➔ **Stop in front of Number 412. Read on to the base of page 35.** (You are in a good place to find out more about the curved Colonnade ahead and the Hotwells Pump Room which formerly adjoined it.)

The *Colonnade* was built in 1786 – with a variety of small shops it must have been Bristol's earliest shopping mall! The upper floors were let as lodgings to visitors to the Hotwell Spa.

In its heyday Ann Yearsley (*1752-1806*) the so-called Milkmaid Poet ran a popular lending library here.

How would you like to live in a cliff side house like one of these? You go in on the ground floor but come out on the **top** floor to reach the *gorge-eous* steep garden. Downstairs is a real cave, at one time a kitchen. What did they bake for tea? Genuine **rock cakes** of course!

The original lease of the hot well was granted in 1695 by the Merchant Venturers who owned the land. The first *Pump House* of 1696 and its early nineteenth-century successor were both built here on a promontory of rock

Answer 16

To tighten ships' ropes to secure them to the quay. Bars were slotted into the capstan and pushed round by strong men. Heave ho!

Answer 17

Cannons. Perhaps they came from a Royal Naval warship, a captured enemy ship or even a real pirate ship. Shiver me timbers!

jutting out into the *Avon* river which was later removed to allow increasingly larger ships to navigate the narrow river more easily. Imagine the wealthy visitors who flocked to the spa from far and wide during the 1700s. As well as people coming to socialize, flirt, dance and gamble, it attracted people seeking a cure for tuberculosis and for other diseases as well. One physician claimed that the milky white waters cured *hot livers, feeble brains and pimply faces!* Local doctors made a very healthy living attending to the invalids who were advised to drink as many as twelve glasses a day. The water was so sought after that it was bottled and exported.

▲ **The old Hot Well House and Spa**
*c.*1804 by W.M.Turner

Answer 18

Two kings. One has a fine moustache.

The Heyday of the Hotwell Spa

Rolinda Sharples lived with her mother at Number 372 St Vincent's Parade, in the background of the painting. Trees obscure the spa which was being rebuilt when this painting was made. It was exhibited at the Royal Academy in 1822 where it was acclaimed. It incorporates many of Rolinda's friends and neighbours. She died in 1838. Her mother bequethed funds to set up the Royal West of England Academy, Bristol.

▲ **Hot Well Spa** c.1855 Built 1696, rebuilt 1822, demolished 1867. Note Brunel's unfinished bridge.

For those lucky enough to visit the Hotwell for sheer pleasure rather than a cure, life was one long social whirl. However, all visitors were expected to abide by strict rules of the Spa's Assembly Rooms imposed by the Master of Ceremonies. These included that *No gentleman appear with a sword or with spurs in these rooms, or on a ball night in boots.*

The old Hotwell House became an obstacle to a new road to Clifton which opened in 1820. The buildings were pulled down and replaced with a neo-classical style in 1822 (above). In 1850 an engineer, James Bolton tried to revive the failing fortunes of the spa by installing a new suite of baths. He sold Hotwells water by the bottle or at 3d a glass and Hotwell tooth powders. Souvenirs were available which even included boomerangs.

◀ **Rownham Ferry**, *c*1820-22,
detail from an oil painting by Rolinda Sharples (*1793-1838*).

▲ **The Pump Room**
Thomas Rolandson
(1756-1827)

For variety we go down to the Bristol spring... and there we drink the water... the ships and boats going up and down the river, close under the windows of the Pump Room, afford such an enchanting variety of moving pictures.

Humphry Clinker by Tobias Smollet (1721-1771)

Bottom station

Bristol diamonds

➔ Now walk down the steps. Proceed with care. A plaque on the Colonnade describes its history. Continue past the former entrance to the Clifton Rocks Railway. This was built by Sir George Newnes in 1893. It ran through a gas lit tunnel 300 feet/152 metres long, carrying passengers between the Hotwells tram terminus and nearby pleasure boat quays to Clifton at the top. It operated on a hydraulic system.

What a pity that the railway cannot still whisk you up to the top of the gorge in 40 seconds as it once did. Instead you can take the healthy option and climb the breathtaking Zig-Zag path.

Continue along passing a small cavern in the cliff. In 1867 the last Hotwell house was demolished and the spa water piped to a pump here. Despite the main spring being closed off, on frosty days look out for a plume of steam rising from the muddy river bank below.

The Zig-Zag path. Time to climb! Take the steep path up. Pause as you reach the first bend in the path. For centuries the gorge was quarried for its limestone. We know from old paintings that vast quantities were removed. Look out for pieces of quartz in the rock face close to you. In the past these were polished and sold to visitors to the Hotwell as Bristol Diamonds. They resembled real gemstones. Records describe jewellery made from them yet strangely none seems to exist today. Across the river you will see the tunnel on the Bristol-Portishead railway line which opened in 1867. It is now used to carry freight inland from the modern Royal Portbury Dock near Portishead, where the *River Avon* meets the Bristol Channel.

As you climb, listen! Can you hear the birds singing? Nuthatches, chiffchaffs, bullfinches, great tits, song thrushes and noisy jays nest here. You might catch sight of a fox – many live in the gorge and venture up to Clifton on their nights out.

Did you know?

The first path up the gorge lead from behind The Colonnade to Prince's Lane. There were 200 steps. The current gentler path was opened in 1849. These steep ways were the shortest routes to Clifton until the opening of the Rocks Railway. It provided the pleasant option of a seated ride until the railway closed in 1934.

You will have an extraordinary view of Brunel's Suspension Bridge high above you.

▲ **The Suspension Bridge**
Started 1831
Completed 1864

The iron links are stretched over the two towers and anchored deep in the solid rock at both ends. The roadway is suspended by rods from these iron links. Before the bridge was built, an iron bar was hauled high across the gorge and a basket hung from it. Mr Brunel and a small boy climbed in and were the first to be pulled across the vast gap. The basket was later used to carry building materials for the bridge. Imagine being that little boy!

At last you reach the top of the *Zig-Zag* path. We said it would be breath-taking!

Caught in a Heavy Shower

Before the Leigh Woods abutment of the Suspension Bridge could be built some rock blasting was necessary. No prior warnings were given! Local papers raised concern that walkers on the Zig-Zag path risked being showered by flying rocks.

Sion Hill to Clifton Down Road

This is **Sion Hill**. The top station of the *Rocks Railway* is to your right, by the ornate railings. It is sometimes open to the public. The right-hand building opposite *Sion Spring House* (c 1780) was built as a new spa when a warm spring similar to that in Hotwells was discovered. Sadly it proved unsuccessful. Look at the grand houses of Sion Hill which provided lodgings to visitors to the spas spanning many years. Take a well-earned break at *The Lookout*. Enjoy the spectacular view of the bridge, 75 metres (245 feet) above river level, designed in 1831 by Isambard Kingdom Brunel. Sadly he died before the bridge was finished and it was completed by his fellow engineers as a memorial to him in 1864. **Question 19**

The bridge chains look delicate but they are very strong and formed from 4,200 iron links each 7.3m x 18cm (24ft x 7ins), weighing 0.51 tonnes (0.5 tons). The chains are up to 51cms (20ins) longer in summer than in winter because heat expands metal.

Take the small footpath along the edge of the gorge towards the bridge. Follow the path round. Across the gorge, is a red-brick Edwardian mansion called *Burwalls*, built in 1872. Nearing the bridge toll house, look up left and you will see the cliff top *Observatory*. On your left are public toilets. Continue along the right-hand pavement of **Suspension Bridge Road**. Detour to playground, see page 2. Walk to the road junction at the top of Sion Hill. Cross it to walk down **Sion Place**. The large building here is Victorian *Bridge House*, a former hotel, now flats. Turn left along a small cobbled footpath. Go past the pub with its six-sided lamp, into **Gloucester Street**. After the first two houses on your right, above a strangely angled doorway, is the inscription *Carter's Buildings*. These buildings are an early version of a Victorian mixed-use development. They provided both storage for traders and housing for those who served the wealthier classes living in the grand houses nearby.

Question 19

Now look at the towers.
Are they the same?

You will reach the **Mall**. Pause here to see opposite a small house, down an alleyway. This is one of the oldest buildings in Clifton. It was once a farm labourer's cottage at a time when the nearby *Coronation Tap* pub was a farmhouse set in tranquil open countryside, far from the bustling city.

➔ Cross the road and turn right down the Mall. At the corner look down. The curb is edged with Victorian cast-iron.
Walk along the left-hand side of **Portland Street**. You pass the exit from Waterloo Street. The buildings there were originally coach houses. Continue. See the decorative scrolls on either side of the entrance to *Elton House*, Number 1, Portland Street, to your right. Reaching **Clifton Down Road** pause to look across at three of Clifton's early grand houses, from left to right, Freemantle, Duncan and Mortimer built in the mid-1700s by wealthy merchants, many of whom had made their fortunes from the Bristol docks below.

▲ **Junction of The Mall with Portland Street**

▼ **Portland Cottage**

Portland Mews, Portland Street, Clifton.
JOHN STONE, JUNIOR,
POST AND JOB MASTER,
LIVERY STABLE KEEPER, ETC.
DOG CARTS, SADDLE HORSES & PONY CARRIAGES, ETC.
HORSES TAKEN IN TO BAIT AND STAND AT LIVERY.
Good Loose Boxes for Hunters. Carriages of all kinds Let on Hire.

From the *Clifton Chronicle* 1850

Rodney Place to Boyce's Avenue

➔ At the end of Portland Street cross right. Pass between the pillars into **Rodney Place**, a terrace of 1785. There are two magnificent trees in the garden, both over a century old. The first is a London Plane and the other a Copper Beech.

Several noted people have lived in the terrace. At Number 2 was Paule Vézelay (*1892-1984*) famous for her abstract paintings. Look at the two plaques at Number 3. One is to Dr Beddoes, who worked in Dowry Square and whose unusual experiments we described earlier. Humphry Davy, his apprentice, also lived here. Beddoes' son, the poet Thomas Lovell Beddoes (*1803-1849*) was another member of the household. The second plaque commemorates John George Lambton, tutored by Dr Beddoes, who later became the first Earl of Durham (*1792-1840*) and first Governor-General of Canada. It was his report in 1830 that led to Canada becoming self-governing. The small lettering on the edge of the plaque records that it was unveiled by the Canadian Prime Minister in 1933.

➔ Return to the main road and walk right to the pedestrian crossing. Cross it, then **Boyce's Avenue**, and you will arrive back at the Clifton Village bus stop where you began your Hotwells walk.

It is not hard to imagine life here in the heyday of the Hotwell. The healthy visitors leaving the newly-built terraces by carriage – perhaps to be served a sumptuous picnic on the Downs and anticipating that evening's grand ball, while others, less fortunate and perhaps dying of consumption, made their weary way once again down to the Hotwell spa to drink the unpleasant waters in the vain hope of a cure. Luckily for you, your cure can be a cup of freshly-brewed tea or coffee in one of Clifton's many delightful cafés.

We hope that you enjoyed your Hotwells and Clifton Village circular walk.

Answer 19

No – the left-hand tower is plain, but the right-hand tower has two spear-shaped openings.

▲ *The Avon from Durdham Down 1829 – detail.*
James Baker Pyne
1800-1870

The Authors

Julia Killingback

A long-term resident who has been much involved in projects promoting this beautiful area. Julia studied art in Bristol (NDD ATD) designing dress textiles in Paris before returning to Bristol to establish her own Studio. Her designs were used on varied products by well-known companies worldwide. Previous published work. Illustrations for 7 Littlest Poetry Books. Author and Illustrator of 12 children's books (Methuen).

Michael Pascoe

Michael Pascoe has made a DVD - "Clifton - a place for all seasons" produced by 1st-Take and a book "The Clifton Guide" published by Redcliffe Press as well as writing many articles on Clifton and Hotwells' rich history. More recently, he co-authored the official guide to the Clifton Suspension Bridge. In 2005 he was awarded the Lord Mayor's medal "for services to Bristol and Clifton".

Acknowledgements:

The authors are most grateful for the goodwill and generosity of the following in helping towards the preparation of this book:

Pippa Gibbs for her kind and attentive editing; Simon Bishop for his expertise in graphic design; Richard Bland's assistance with the flora and fauna and Dawn Dyer (Bristol City Reference Library) for her unfailing help.

Our thanks also go to Anthony Beeson, David Bolton, Ross Floyd, Simon Gibbs, Francis Greenacre, Elfyn Griffith, Alison Lewis, Andy Lillie, Janet Margrie, Tom Mocek, Rose Mary Musgrave, Pim Palmen, John Sleight, Ray Smith, and Sue Stops.

The authors would especially like to thank the individuals, families, friends and children who kindly 'route tested' our walks in all winds and weathers – and approved them! Their comments were invaluable.

Credits

The authors and publishers are most grateful for permission to reproduce the following Illustrations which are © copyright of the organisations or individuals listed:

Key

(PC) = Postcard
L = Left – from top down, then base panel L-R
R = Right – from top down, then base panel L-R
O.U.C out of copyright
(SU)=source unknown
(WU)=whereabouts unknown

Illustrations reproduced by kind permission of the following:

Bristol Central Reference Library (BCRL)
P10 L4; P11R2; P14L2; P20L4 and Base L-R (1-4); P22L4; P26L4; P27R2; P35R2; P38L1

BCRL Newspaper Archives
(A Chronicle of Clifton) P21R3; P39 Base

Copyright Bristol City Museums Galleries and Archives (BMAG)
P6-7; P8-9; P24L3; P33(Main); P34(Base); P41

Clifton Rocks Railway
P36 L1 (PC)

The Clifton Suspension Bridge Trust P29 R3

John Sansom. Redcliffe Press, Bristol
P25 L2 *Bristol's Floating Harbour: The first 200 years.* Peter Malpass and Andy King 2009. P 34(Main W.U) *From Bristol to the Sea.* Francis Greenacre 2005

From private collections
Collage P5 L-R11 "Approach to the Hotwell House "1792 Illustration from Evelina by Fanny Burney (O.U.C)
P22L2; P23 R1; P22 L2; P23 R1; P24L4; P30 L2 (Paddle Steamer-Waverley); P35 R1(PC)
Ruth Packer P30 A14 Thomas Bewick (1753-1828)-Wood Engraving from 1947 King Penguin/Penguin Books inc.

Julia Killingback Illustrations
Collage P5 L-R 2 and P16 L2; P18L2; P22A7; P24A10; A11; P25R1(Birds); P32A17; P37R2

Front & Inside Front Cover
Simon Bishop

Back Cover
The Cumberland Basin in 1850 (detail from "Clifton and the Harbour at Hotwells") Lithograph by E.T. Dolby - Bristol Reference Library

Bristol Mayor George Ferguson
Back cover image of Mayor George Ferguson
The Post www.thisisbristol.co.uk

Wallace & Gromit's Grand Appeal Bristol Children's Hospital Charity Donate (www.grandappeal.org.uk/donate)

Every effort has been made to trace and acknowledge the source of all illustrations included. We would like to apologise for any errors or omissions.

Organisations
Hotwells and Cliftonwood Community Association
The Clifton and Hotwells Improvement Society
Swivel Bridge Restoration Project

Photographs
Most photographs were taken by Julia Killingback and Trevor Palmer. Our thanks also to Simon Bishop P38L2; Gary Thoburn P30L4; Clare Brook P36L3

All images are copyright of the photographers unless otherwise stated.

Series design concept, map and drawn illustrations
© Julia Killingback

Useful contacts
Bristol's Ferry Boats
0117. 9273416
www.bristolferry.com
Number Seven Boat Trips
0117 9293659 / 07976 554024
www.numbersevenboattrips.com

Bus information
www.firstgroup.com/ukbus/bristol

Open Top Bus
www.citysightseeingbristol.co.uk

Hotwells and Cliftonwood Community Association
www.hotwellscliftonwood.org.uk

Clifton and Hotwells Improvement Society
www.cliftonhotwells.org.uk

Brunel Swivel Bridge Restoration Project
www.brunelbridge.org.uk

The Clifton Rocks Railway
www.cliftonrocksrailway.org.uk

Clifton Suspension Bridge
www.cliftonbridge.org.uk

Tourist Information
www.visitbristol.co.uk

Bristol City Museums and Art Gallery
www.bristol.co.uk/museumsandgalleries

Bristol Central Library
www.bristol.gov.uk/libraries

The Create Centre:
0117.9250505
www.createbristol.org

Support funding for this project was kindly provided by Bristol City Council Neighbourhood Partnership Well Being Fund

All information is correct at the time of going to press. The authors cannot be held liable for any changes which may have occurred subsequently.

No part of this book may be reproduced by any means without the permission of the copyright holders.

Text copyright © 2014 Julia Killingback and Michael Pascoe.

Series design concept and drawn illustrations
© 2014 Julia Killingback

First published 2014
by Julia Killingback

EXPLOREWALKS UK
Explorewalks UK
All rights reserved.
Printed by Short Run Press, Exeter
ISBN 978-1-910089-06-4

For our families with love – and for all who delight in taking a step out of the ordinary
JK & MP

4. HOTWELLS

Explore Bristol

EXPLOREWALKS UK

ON FOOT

Other Explorewalks titles in the series

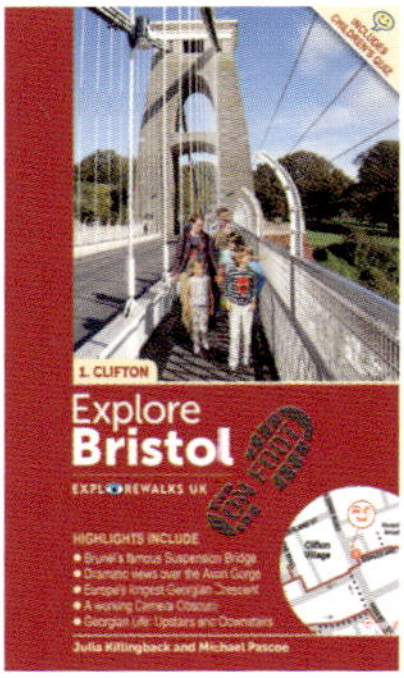

No 1. Clifton

No 2. Victorian Clifton

No 3. Cliftonwood

For information on other walks guides in this series go to

www.explorewalks.co.uk